A Life WELL LIVED THROUGH Words

SHARON D. GREENSPAN

EDITED BY HILLARY M. PRESTON

Order this book online at www.trafford.com
or email orders@trafford.com

Most Trafford titles are also available at major online book retailers.

Printed in the United States of America.

ISBN: 978-1-4907-3412-5 (sc)
ISBN: 978-1-4907-3411-8 (e)

Trafford rev. 05/02/2014

www.trafford.com
North America & international
toll-free: 1 888 232 4444 (USA & Canada)
fax: 812 355 4082

Dedication

For Samantha.

Always follow your dreams, you were my dream and I will always be there for you.

About the Author

Sharon Diane Greenspan is an Immigration Attorney who worked for the U.S. Immigration and Naturalization Service as an Assistant Regional Counsel, in California. Born to immigrant parents, Sharon has always been drawn to the immigrant experience. Before becoming an attorney, she spent two years as a journalist, writing and editing the <u>Illinois Education News,</u> where she won National Press Awards. Her early childhood was spent in the Humboldt Park neighborhood of Chicago. Over the years, she endured challenging relationships, but eventually married Steven and had her daughter Samantha. Her major challenge in life has been battling chronic fatigue syndrome. That was the major reason she retired from full time law practice. Through it all, she has always looked to poetry and other writing to find her peace. Within the following collection of poems, Sharon recounts her experiences and weaves together her own story of a life well lived through words.

Letter from the Editor

To paraphrase Ann Patchett, writing is a craft. It is something you hone after getting all your first attempts out on paper. Not everything you write will be good; not everything you write makes you a writer. It is the practice and the craft of trying that makes you great.

Sharon has been writing for decades, getting everything from raw emotion to words of wisdom out into the written word. But more than that, Sharon is a true storyteller. Drawn from all crucial moments and relationships in her life, these poems are her stories put to paper creating a tantalizing memoir of a life well documented through poetry. I applaud Sharon for reawakening the love of poetry and writing not just within me but for those reading this collection. For those of you who have any inkling or spark of wanting to write—prepare to ignite it.

Hillary Marshak Preston

CONTENTS

MAGICAL MOMENTS THAT CHANGE YOUR LIFE

SEVENTY-FIVE CANDLES ON A CAKE

For the library—institution of public learning—
seventy-five candles are a tribute, an achievement.
It incorporates the notion that we are immortal,
Through our words.

When we humans,
Go to blow out our birthday candles,
If there <u>are</u> *seventy-five*—we think of all those years,
Life is winding down.

Why does the library live and age so gracefully?
It is a home—to the words of mystical-angel inspired,
writers, poets, jokers, illustrators—
who imbue their creative spirit energy into print,
and colored pictures, and novels.
To the poor and desolate,
the abused and bemused;
it is the ability to take us away.

Ah, the smells and touches of the library.
The feel of a well-worn <u>Huckleberry Finn,</u>
Or my pre-adolescent <u>Nancy Drew Detective</u>
The ever-present joy when I read to my one and only daughter,
"I'll love you forever—
As long as I'm living my baby you'll be."

Feel the first experiments at curling up
in a library to do research:
First research paper in high school,
Then college, law school,
Studying for the bar exam in the library.
Savor those memories.

Our great television personality with her "Use Your Life" series,
marvels at how books saved her—made her
(a small black girl from Mississippi),
believe she could be anyone she wanted to be!

Now, she has millions reading about all parts of the world
they would never be exposed to otherwise.
Publishers herald her—
she has re-inspired book sales, book clubs, and libraries.

Some people feel the coffeehouses and bookstores
have replaced the library,
they are mistaken.
No history or the aura of old souls.
It is no coincidence, that, in the movie,
City of Angels, Nicolas Cage (an angel), hung out at the
Los Angeles Public Library.

Remember the Twilight Zone with a main character
who only wanted to be left alone to read?
There is a nuclear holocaust, everything is desolate:
He wakes up alive in the rubble, with books all around him
At first he is ecstatic.
Then, the horrific irony—his glasses are smashed.
He can't read.
Our libraries and books need us as much as we need them.

From generation to generation,
In all stages of our growing up,
One could always find a book to elucidate on the subject;
Adolescence, Dating, Getting Married, Parenting,
Speaking to your kids of adolescence,
Taking care of your parents,
How to find good doctors, build houses, buy cars,
Find the right spiritual home.

Through books we learned of John, and Bobby and Martin,
We learned of Adolf Hitler—and the eyes and ears
and heart of Elie Wiesel.
We had Sendak and his wild things, and Little Women,
and Laura Ingalls on the Prairie.

We must remember in this land of the free—
How *we are free* to have libraries.
In Afghanistan, and Iran books are banned.
In India, there are no public libraries.
So many immigrants talk of their first experience of
Coming to America and being able to "borrow" *free of charge*
A library book.

In America we celebrate milestones.
We honor our birthdays and our anniversaries.
We know that, there but for the grace of G-d go I.

The cake should be big, big, big,
The banners should be big, big, and big
Shout from the rooftops,
We Deerfieldtonian readers are 75 years old.
We made it. We're going to live to be 200.
Our books are our *gifts* from our ancestors,
and *legacy* to our descendants.

Hail! Hail! Long shall we read.

© Sharon D. Greenspan, 2002.
Original work received an Honorable Mention in the Rosemary Sazonoff
Creative Writing Contest at the Deerfield Public Library, Deerfield, Illinois.

I DANCED ON OPRAH

I Danced on Oprah,
Fifteen minutes of fame . . .
Nothing else in life quite as big.

Freshman year in college,
the Dean of Women Students
at Northern Illinois University wanted to meet me.
She had me to her office for tea
She said I had one of the highest IQs at the school.
Huh?

But that, wasn't as big as Dancing on Oprah.
Top ten percent of my law school class
wasn't as big as Dancing on Oprah.
Never shy or retiring; so thrilled to get a seat at the Oprah show.
It was the midyears, 1997?
No friends to accompany me to the Oprah show.
Ridiculous people wanted to know if it was a giveaway show.
Priorities.

But no, I went because I sold a Producer on my Parenting Philosophy.
"What's that, you say?"
I said, the less you say NO between 1 and 5 . . .
the less you'll have to say NO between 13 and 18.
The world will knock our kids down enough
We have to build them up.
So I went to the Oprah show.

But then, switcheroo.
They were taping three shows.
One was a promo for <u>Dance With Me</u> (the movie)

There, in a Robin's egg gorgeous blue dress
was Vanessa Williams.
Sitting in a chair next to a Latin heartthrob
whose name was Cheyenne.
He was not yet famous in America.

Oh, what a story!
How is this possible?
I know as much about Latin dancing as parenting.

Cheyenne and Vanessa danced.
Oprah came and sat in the audience directly in front of me.
Oprah said something like—
"Cheyenne wants me to dance with him.
I'm not going to do what it took Vanessa Williams six months to learn.
I'm not going to make myself a fool in front of millions of people."

I am too impulsive. I am too unfiltered.
I leaned forward, tapped Oprah on the shoulder and said
"Oprah, my dad is 78 and he still does Latin dancing all over Chicago
and I was taught to do mambo, cha-cha, and rumba when I was 10
AND IT'S NOT THAT HARD!"

Next thing I know, a microphone is in my face.
Then I was on a stage.
I salsa-ed with Cheyenne.
I was a sensation.
They called me the Salsa Lady.

Those ten minutes, more important than getting a law degree?
More important than having a certificate
from the Attorney General of the United States?

Samantha, the lovechild, was five.
She did not yet know who Oprah was.
At school, she found out.

Later, they called it the Oprah effect.

© Sharon D. Greenspan, 2014.
*(This poem was written 17 years later, and I'm still an Oprahphile,
Go OWN!)*

We speak of hearts
   In the love equation.
Hearts pump the blood, life force,
Lips are the entryway to life, souls and mind.

The on-screen kiss
   That we sense is real—
The flutter that sends tingles from our lips
   through our entire cell structure.

And the heavenly must play a part
for love is truly the moving of my soul
   through yours,
on the wings of cupid's arrow.

We are "drunk with desire."
We swagger; our heads spin.
Our entire culture yearns for romantic crazy
   LOVE.
We want to be like "Rose"
   when she catapulted from the life raft,
   back onboard the Titanic to be with "Jack".

How many of us have felt that life or death love—
of Capulet and Montague fame?

My mother and father had that Romeo-and-Juliet-like electricity.
They loved each other with passion befitting a torrential rain,
   a Spanish bullfight, a Latin *Merengue. Quick, slow, quick, slow,*
   Undulating hips.
From the moment they met—he,
the Casanova, Jewish **Ricky** Ricardo—could not
give up his beautiful Jewish Viennese Sali **Lucy.**

Having grown up with passionate parents,
And parent's friends with
    numbers on their arms.
I saw many examples of enduring love.
They could not speak of the horrors of the death camps;
But they could sing and glorify in their love for one another—
Having found one another out of the ashes.

The love these survivors showered on their children,
    is a very different love.
It is tinged with the suffering of loss,
for they have understood the frailty of life.

The love I feel for my aging parents is so strong—
I sometimes feel as if I shall overflow.

Having to say goodbye to my father
    on a hospital bed,
My heart cried through my lips,
"Daddy, I love you, please don't leave me."
I cherish all the days left with my Mama.

The love I feel for my Samantha—baby of my forties,
There are no parallels.
It is as if two hearts beat as one.
She has an earache; my ear swells.
She receives an award, my arm rises to touch it in the audience.
I suppose my immortality lies within her.

The day of her birth—
I could only think of the truly highest love . . .
The infinite love of G-d, the Creator, the universe,
for giving me the blessing of a child.

But alas,
romantic love,
Has not been my forte.
It is elusive.
Lovers have come and gone.
Some have stayed too long
Love must change and grow,
Spiral upward or it dies.
How do we grow to understand one another,
When we don't have the same blood chemistry?
So we come full circle, the intertwining of souls.
Thus spoke the Little Prince:
"It is the time you have wasted on your rose
that makes her important,"
"Only with the heart that one can see rightly."
"What is essential is invisible to the eye."

So with every breath I take,
Heart keep on pumping!

ON POETRY AND WRITING

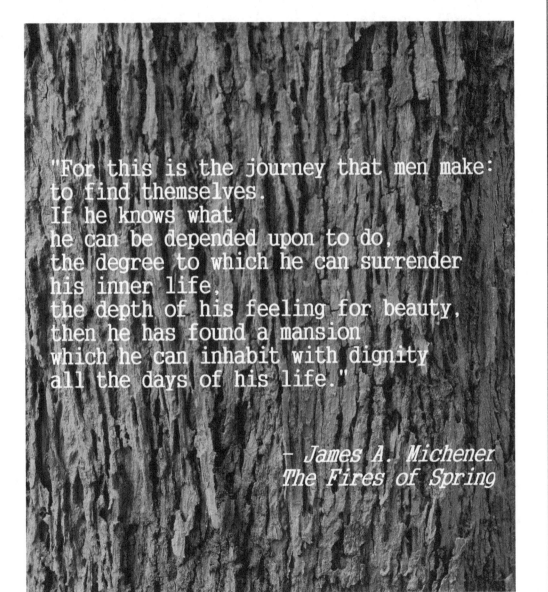

"For this is the journey that men make:
to find themselves.
If he knows what
he can be depended upon to do,
the degree to which he can surrender
his inner life,
the depth of his feeling for beauty,
then he has found a mansion
which he can inhabit with dignity
all the days of his life."

– James A. Michener
The Fires of Spring

RIDING THE WAVES

The stories are always with me,
Begging to be spoken, written,
immortalized before forgotten.
A poem is a fleeting memory,
It must be captured in its fullness,
when it is rising.

The surfer waits for the wave
    and rides it
The poet waits for the words,
    patiently
    then *swoosh*!

A PLEA FROM THE POET

Sweet violins, sadly stringing, melodies,
tunes, sonatas, singing—the heart.

Reaching, searching, sorrowful sweet,
Ah! Music, man's minstrely sweet protégé.
To you we turn, in time of sadness,
For music sings the sorrows of the heart,
very rarely the joys.

To create, make a whole, spiraling towards the sky,
out of separate disjointed parts.
Like trees swaying to nature's songs,
So I sway, in this hour of melancholy,
to the soft, sweet sound of the old masters,
who knew suffering oh so well.

He had not ears, yet he could hear,
not the words, but the ideas,
which were oh so more important.

I have ears, yet I can not hear,
what those mute organs could,
Yet I tried to play the suffering of the soul,
in words,
creating, dissecting, helping, and constantly trying,
To obtain those dear perfections which only they knew.

TO JOHN STEINBECK
(ABOUT *JOURNEY OF A NOVEL*)

Little did you know John,
When you wrote those notes along with your book,
where they would wind up.

Little did you know, that the book you thought
   would be shunned, dissected by critics,
Warmed the hearts of all, and was loved by all.

Your book,
Beautiful, filling the empty cavity of the heart,
with all the words, which may not really be the
exact ones . . .
Yet you were enough of a master to come close.

And you filled your box,
Of stories, of life, and death, and hate and love,
and light and darkness, and all the paradoxes of man,
   which we all know and loved so well.
Of blood lines, and free will, and destiny, and eternity,
and now.
Of suffering, and ecstasy . . .
All for your little boys to read, when they were no
   longer little.

And I, a little girl, no longer little, stumbled
upon your beautiful box full of treasures,
   and learned also the beautiful paradox of life,
and brothers, and G-d and truth and right . . .
No longer afraid . . . for *TIMSHEL*.

G-d said "I give you a blessing and a curse."
If you love the commandments with your heart and do them
 they will be a blessing.
If you do the commandments merely out of duty, they will
 be a curse.

Thou mayest choose . . . *Timshel*.

ON POETRY

Oh, my friend,
I return to your keys so lovingly.
It has been such a long time
since there was anything inside to be said.

Why is it that only in times of extreme pain, I feel poetry?
Is it the hurt which re-sensitizes us to feel again?

When I am happy, there are few words of poetry.
There is contentment, and no reason to speak.
It is only in times like this, times of agony where to say
my heart is broken is an understatement.
It feels as if my insides have been scattered
all across the universe, with no resting place,
and no way to bring them all together.

It's like an image of a vacuum cleaner, suck up all my parts,
clean away all of my dirt, make me whole again.
I wish there were a vacuum cleaner in my life,
someone who could put me back together again.
Or better yet a glue that never comes apart again.

Images, images, of being lost and lonely and alone,
and no where to run,
no one to turn to, but the comfort of words.

THE GYPSY LADY

That's right, poker face, deal.
No one will ever really know,
Is he bluffing?

Except the gypsy lady,
She looks in her crystal ball,
and she knows all.

Little Susie sweetie,
Sweets not meant for eating,
Is she cheating, or isn't she?
No one will ever know.

Except the gypsy lady,
She looks in her crystal ball,
and she knows all.

And here comes Father McCann,
Tall, thin straight, and angelic.
But no one really knows,
If he's really pure, or just a brass relic.

Except the gypsy lady,
She looks in her crystal ball,
and she knows all.

And the poet, ah, he tries to hide,
No one will really know the meaning inside,
I can write anything I want,
Without ever having to expose my thoughts.

Except the gypsy lady,
She looks in her crystal ball,
and she knows all.

Gypsy lady—What are you hiding?

VULNERABILITY

Vulnerability.
The world rolls on my tongue and through my system
as grease through an engine.
The ability to be vulnerable.
I'm vulnerable.

Hit me in my vulnerability.
"He got her when she was vulnerable"
We're all talking about it as I write to hold back the tears
hoping the water won't smear the ink.
Creative genius—you're brilliant when you're angry.

My swords of words are so sharp they sparkle
and shatter all they come into contact with.
Vulnerability.

POETRY IS NOT GOOD ENOUGH

Everyone tells her:
Give up the poetry
Who reads that stuff anyway?

Write your book.
Immigration is all over the news.
Everyone wants to hear what you have to say.

Yeah, right.
I'm a genie in a bottle.
Let's see—I'll stay up all night,
in between taking care of my teen daughter,
paying the bills,
filling out the forms,
still tying up loose ends from the loss of my mother,
sniffling from one cold to the other.

Sure, I'm not disabled.
I'm not well enough to practice law,
but I'll just write a book.

Yeah, the women who lunch
in my book club—they want some royalties if
I write a book.
They can't even contribute to pay for me to be their
leader to the book club.
But I'll write a book, and give them all the credit.

Yeah, they helped me get here.
No one helps you get anywhere.
Oh sure, here's a how-to guide, or I'll edit, or
whatever.

But I have yet to find my Mitch Albom.
I want to talk like *Tuesdays with Morrie*.
I am fatigued. I can't write it all myself.
I can only write one poem at a time.

Someone come for my words, before my brain,
and my lips cannot form them.

Ah, dear, bring me your words,
I am safe—I shall not hurt you.
My touch of pen shall be gentle, encourage, love, listen,
Give me your sheaf of papers—your poetry hand.
She hesitates—thinking, dreaming, glorifying,
remembering he who hesitates is lost . . .

She hands the envelope over—please read, advise.
In between she dreams of readings, and awards, and adoring fans,
and a legacy of uplifting words . . .

Then, it is KRISTALLNACHT.
Shards of glass fly, German shepherds bear fangs, saliva dripping—
ready to pounce on her flesh.
TERRIBLE, *muy mala, hey-lee baad*, bad in twenty seven languages.
Nicht gut.

This is not a warm mother. Mamas brush back one's hair—
Encourage you to fly—'defy gravity' as the song goes.
Instead, "Shouldn't have offered to read," she says.
"The words are so bad they hurt my eyes—
you wasted my precious time!"

The shards of glass open old wounds;
I shall walk the stations of the cross.
The gigantic nail in my forehead oozes red,
and the green of envy.
My palms are no longer red or read.

Beware of friends bearing gifts,
the apple becomes poisonous,
razor sharp, like glass to the tongue—
Do not come this way again.

PAPER THE WALLS WITH POETRY

Paper the walls with poetry,
And the stalls with poetry,
I want my pants to dance with poetry,
Slide down that street with poetry.

If you write it, they will come.

THE IMMIGRANT EXPERIENCE:
MY LIFE AND TIMES AS
AN ATTORNEY

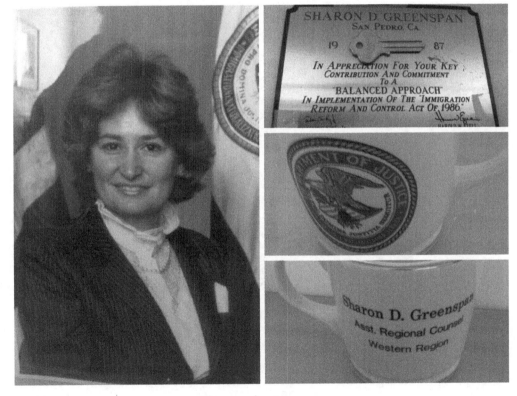

Sharon, the Attorney.

THE LAWYER

So I have become someone new,
I speak, I think, I react
   with reason.
My emotion and passion are being funneled,
funneled to fuel your disputes.
Your pettiness.
And occasionally your sense of justice.

Although I strive to only involve myself in the latter.
The reality of the marketplace brings me into contact with the former.
But yet it is service.
If I can mend one soul, save one conscience,
adopt one child,
bring one new immigrant to this land of freedom,
free one man wrongfully accused,
then it shall be worth it.

LOVE IN THE TIME OF THE
IMMIGRATION SERVICE

It was a magical place.
Others hated it.
But I walked in and
fell in love with
The United States Immigration Service.

Brand new, sparkly spanking clean
pretty young attorney
not quite 30.
New boss; *shyster* lawyer.
Hard for girls to get jobs.

He was only interested in the clients' accident cases.
Plenty of them.
That's where the money is.

"Here," he shoved an inch leaf of papers at her.
"Figure out how to handle this stuff!"

Clients asking for help.
"Bring my family . . ."
Not across the border that we scream about now—
but from the other side of the world—
The Middle East.
My ancestors hailed from there 2,000 years before
but not from my side of the Middle East, from the other side.
A-ha, the learning begins.

The European boss is an anti-Semite.
Not so the clients.
Iraqi-Assyrians, Lebanese-Christians, Armenians, and Iranians
love the idea of a smart Jewish lawyer.

I fill up papers
I walk the two blocks to the mammoth Federal building.
I walk in, the huge information desk is in the center of the lobby.

A line,
longer than any concert line I have ever seen,
Is snaked around the whole lobby.

All types of dress; *saris,* American boots, *turbans,*
hijabs, kippot, bright colored island wear,
and languages a million.
I have found my brood.
My children flock.
Give me your tired, your poor,
your huddled masses breathing to be free.

THE NAME GAME

Let's play the name game.
What's in a NAME CHANGE?
Is it only name shame?
A rose by any other name is the same.
(She changed her name as immigrants do.)

Wanted to be more like me and you.
Plus, it's free . . .
In America, a name change is free.

FREE to be you and me.
FREE from sea to shining sea.
FREE when you become a U.S.C.
United States Citizen, that is.

So my mommy, my *muter, meine liebshun,*
wanted to be more American.
In childhood, in *Vien*, they teased her, bullied her,
Sali—was a boy's name—pronounced "Solly".

But in America, Sali—
or Sally was of Dick and Jane fame.
SALLY was a great name.
First readers had Sallys.

Hey nowadays we have Sally Mae.
She didn't know . . .
So my *Yiddishe mama* in her infinite wisdom
changed her name to—
SYLVIA!—SYLVIA?
A hot mama, Latin dancer of the fifties?
Better to be a Latina than a German Jew?

SYLVIA NMN GREENSPAN
Oh yea, the NMN for those of you unfamiliar:
No Middle Name.

A rose by any other name
Good old Sali, became Sylvia.

DORIS DAY

Give me your tired, your hungry, your poor.
Give me your name.

She was beautiful.
A dark Middle Eastern beauty,
A platinum Marilyn Monroe.

Blonde, Sex and The City high heels before <u>Sex and The City</u>
From a 5,000 year old Assyrian culture.
The officer said "You sure you want to change your name?"
"I'm sure" she smiled, shaking her head.
Showing her newly white brightened teeth.

"Ok, what would you like your name to be?" the officer asked.
He continued, "Your current name is Itamara Shmuel"
She brightened, "TAMMY ADAMS!"
"I want to be Tammy Adams!"

And the Lord looked down and saw that it was good.

PERSIAN PRINCESS

I am a Persian Princess
Not an *Ojibwan*
Nor an Ethiopian
Nor a Moroccan . . .

A Persian Princess
My essence has lived in the
time of Cyrus the Great.
The scent of saffron,
and sumac transport
me to my previous life.

Salaam, Shalom
I am a Persian Hebrew Princess.
Happy in my Hebrewness
Proud of my Persianness

Nowruz is the beginning of the year March 20th.
heralds the coming of spring
and the new year
My passage of birth to
this world took place on
March 23rd.

I was welcomed here with *Nowruz*.
In my dreams I see the *Nowruz haft-seen* table.

Fill me with the delicate tea,
sipping from a beautiful gold rimmed glass,
a cube of *ghand* in between my teeth.
Persian gastronomy.
Khoreshts, sabzis, and tahdigs.

The land of Hafez and Rumi.
Of minarets and mosaic sparkling blue tiles and pistachios.

The language calls me in the night.

Beh-rim, Raftam,
Let's go.
Magic carpet let's fly to my Persian home of yore,
some day I shall once again lay my head
in the lap of my Persian Prince.
Looking out at the Caspian sea.

LOVE, LOVE, LOVE . . .

FRIEND OR FOE

Like a medieval castle I stand,
with only my moat separating us.
I could let the bridge down and let you in,
but first I have to be quite sure,
whether you are friend or foe.

All you have to say are the magic words,
the code . . . It's not that hard.
Search your heart. Is there bitterness there?
Is there love?
Are you friend or foe?

Maybe I'll let down my drawbridge,
But caution; once inside this castle,
you will never return to the forest again;
at least not alone.

SONNET I

With what great care I run to you,
Like a child, weeping, kind and true.
Only to be reassured of this,
That you will help me with a kiss,
For man does not live all alone,
He carries a helper in the bone.

To me you are my needed saint,
Without your love, I would surely faint,
So help me please to see again,
And take away this aching pain.
For the truth to me is surely clear,
Before your eyes, I wasn't here.

IN THE TROPICS

His words,
flowed through the soft Caribbean night,
with the strength of his new body
walking next to hers.

"Have you ever been in love?"
A question answered before spoken . . .
Words swell within her throat
"Now, only now."

She has known this voice, face,
    eyes and hands but a few hours
Yet she has known them always.

There is a change
A knowledge
    that now that his soul has
    moved within hers,
An empty space was filled, but
    another created.

THE PERSIAN KING

It's the nights,
I can't give up the nights.
You were gone a month—I didn't sleep
Not without the bedroom door blocked
Listening for every sound
Thinking it was your foot on the steps.

And last night you were back
No one understands how I take you back
All the time
It's because I never saw eyes like mine before
They always told me "you have incredible eyes"
Deep brown pools, magical, enchanting—
But you have my eyes
And your smile—charm the world with that smile.

Cruel—
"I'm getting married tomorrow, do you want to come?"
"Who is she?"
"You know her."
"I do?"
"Yes, she says she knows you."
"Be at the Sheraton at eight o'clock."

"How can you marry someone you've known for a few weeks?
I gave you two years, my life, my time, my soul—
Literally I died for you—marry me!"

Something died in me when you said you were going to marry.
When I cried, begged for forgiveness, for your love, you said,
"No I'm only kidding. I'm not getting married yet."
I wanted to race the clock.
To stop you, like Dustin in The Graduate,
"Elaine, Elaine, Elaine"

King, King, I love you too much,
but yet I know you destroy me.

Life is a circle, with pockmarks.
G-d, please help me find the answers.
When will I finally say no, or
Yes, Yes, Yes, forever.

CALIFORNIA DREAMING

The wind wafted through the
   room,
Tinkling the blinds,
She stirred—
Feeling the gentle breeze.
A lover's yawn,
toss, stretch like a cat.
The day is here,
She's not ready for it.
She's still in the night.
With him.

DISSONANCE

Our melodies are harsh, sounding off-key,
the tones of our souls no longer harmonizing
Dissonance,
Will we ever find the harmony again?

Lovers walk,
the strings of their bodies synchronized,
silly smiles swaying with the wind.

We're like a G sharp and an F, never meant to be played together.

MOONLIGHT SHIVERS

Daytime dreams,
Nighttime horrors.
Frightened screams,
Pale dead floors.

The moonlight shivers the lace,
in the ladies' star-filled room.
She lies alone,
her rumpled bed her only protection
Against,
the ghosts of dreams and memories
    that haunt the soul.
The haunted house.

She longs to hear the clickety-clack.
Her lovers sound through the night.
As he rides over the cobblestones to meet her.
She knows, but she refuses to admit.
He is far away, on a distant shore,
where the only sounds are clashing
of swords and gunshots screaming.
And she waits,
not knowing there is someone else waiting
    for her love . . .

I'D LIKE TO KNOW . . .

I'd like to know,
just where your heart lies,
And if there's just a little room,
For me to lie there too.

Rivers of sadness,
Teardrops of longing,
Haven't kept us apart as much,
as decades of indifference.
I'd rather you say you hate
then "I don't care."

IN AN INSTANT

He changed the geography of the bed,
The continents of sheets rearranged,
Now an island here, an isthmus there.

No longer a single shimmer of land in the middle,
straddling two sides, trying to make a two out of a one.
She was no longer stranded.

No he did not gallop in on a white horse to save her,
Nor was he a knight in shining armor.
Just a strong, serene, steady oarsman,
who came ashore,
and changed the geography of the bed.

INSPIRATION

It has been many months
yet you inspire me
to write it, rather than say . . .
I used to write.

The visions are very clear.
I shall not be distracted
by wine, old movies, or peanuts;
sensitive, natural, basic.

You are a man, of a different culture.
But yet I have never fit with a man of my own.
The edges have never interwoven.
Sometimes it seems as though I am of another
    time and culture
dispersed physically from my time.

The beauty of poetry becomes ineffectual,
    tired, out of tune when unused.
My style, my expression, are as the guitar in the
    corner—
Dusty and warped.

But I shall return my guitar, my soul,
    my words, expression and verse . . .
For you . . .
    inspire me.

DIMPLES

Ah, the newness of a new love.
The color, depth, intensity of the eyes,
The shape of the nose, and expression
    of the mouth.
Searching the face to find the dimple,
    or the scars.

And the words flow,
On and on into the night.
"No, I didn't want to see a movie"
"I wanted to talk to get to know you."
"You are very wise," he said.
Simplistic compliments that soothe the pain
    that turn the scars back into dimples.

TO MY LOST HUSBAND

I

I could say I don't care,
but you haunt me.

People tell me I talk like you,
walk like you.
I lost myself in you.
Now you're gone.
And I don't know where I am.

II

I wondered, and now I know,
As you speak words to me,
and you glimmer with my appreciation and approval,
I now know what she gave him,
Which I could not.
Not because I wasn't able,
Not because the words weren't there,
But because I was who I was,
I was Wife.

And likewise, she will never again be
able to give to you the love you
need to flower, nor the appreciation
because you are and always will be
My husband.

III

These are the first words I will write to you,
or of you since your death.
Yes death; death and divorce are the same
words with different spellings.

They all tell me—let him fly, he's confused,
he doesn't know who he is,
but he loves you, or no, he doesn't really love you.

There really will never be anyone to replace you.
When Romeo found Juliet dead, he didn't say
'Well I'll wait a few years and find a new love.'
He killed himself right there and then.

I do envy you.
You don't seem to hurt as I do.
Are you as lost as I?
It's not as if you want someone else,
for right now you just don't want me.

When I saw you on the street, my defenses were down.
It was so unexpected;
I just wanted to go up to you and give you a hug and a kiss,
as if you had just come home from a hard day's work.

Is it because I didn't build you up enough?
Was I not understanding enough?
I suppose that I hadn't yet learned how to let you feel big,
without me feeling small.
I didn't know what a wife was supposed to be.
To stand next to; but a few steps behind.

Will there ever be a time for us again? Is this the real last time?
How long can we go on like this?
Do you think you can ever find someone who
can love you as much as me?

Ah, the sorrows of young Werther.

IV

Shadows follow me,
Memories drowning my senses.

How can I ever begin to tell you?
How my heart is so sensitive,
it weeps with the rain,
it floats with the clouds.

You put a chain on yours
It begs to weep,
you scorn it.

It begs to float, to love
you abuse it.

Love me again,
You who taught me how to love,
how to live in another.
How to give.

V

It's all welled up inside
To feel from within,
      and me stifled from without.

I've failed.

I so much wanted
    to be
something
something worth your love.

I wanted to be there
    to reflect you, think with you,
    see with you, make love with you

But
    I've failed.

To you
    I'm not more than a wing cutter.

I cut off your wings,
    Took away your freedom.
    I clipped your wings.

© Sharon D. Greenspan, late 1970s.

A FEW AROUND . . .

There is someone new in my life,
He kind of crept in slowly.
He doesn't know yet the effect he had made
on the fear.

I desire to believe that he's as good as he seems.
Or to believe the words he says
but I am afraid.

Afraid to believe that I can let someone close
And they won't leave.

That's why I juggle.
I have to keep a few around.
So if one leaves there are others
to turn to.

BUS STOP

The dream is usually the same
Which way does this bus go?
Is it the suburban bus of my teen years,
that transports me to the mall or library?

I get lost—buses and terminals are mixed up.
It's Amsterdam, London, Rome, Paris,
Not sixteen anymore, now over a half century old,
Still unsure which bus to take . . .
The bus ride to California dreaming lasted seven years,
And had to take a train home to the Prairie State.

Not paying attention, not caring works in youth.
Now I sweat, anxiety racing up my body,
The sign on top of the bus keeps changing, scrolling,
"Get on board, can't wait all day," the driver yells.
Who cares if you're confused, or can't move too quickly . . .
How come I couldn't fast forward in my teens, and see this?

Wish the dream had a final destination—an end of the line,
beautiful with the lush hyacinths and a knight in shining armor.
The *one* who got lost—trying to keep up with all those buses.
We'd board the bus together for 'Happily ever after'
Skin tight, hair flowing with no signs of gray,
Last stop—all is well in the world.
No more dreams, the right bus has arrived.

© Sharon D. Greenspan, 2001.

PHONE STATIC

How does it cycle out of control?
A sweet sensitive voice,
Now screech, a shrill kettle whistling.

Talking at the other across phone space.
Eavesdroppers wouldn't know how it started.
Epithets, swearwords, tears; two years old.

Throw down my toy and go home.
Step back into the ring for the last punch.
The last word. Deep breath; diffuse.

Our commonality is our love child.
What we once had, now a faded memory.
The subject matter doesn't matter.

*This poem was printed in the poetry compilation **Tracing the Infinite: The International Library of Poetry,** released in 2004.*

SOUL SORES

A romantic evening,
The two of us sat in our
Whirlpool tub.
Each of us resting our
backs against the opposite side.

My soaked feet crawled
up his chest.
He started massaging
my feet.

"You know," I said.
"All any woman wants is a man who makes her soul soar."

He looked at me with a
question in his eyes.
Still massaging my feet.

"I don't get it", he said.
"You don't get what?" I replied.

Why would a woman
want a man who makes
her feet hurt?

Sole sore?
Soul soar?

Women are from Venus.
Men are from Mars.

THE BODY REMEMBERS

Eyes closed, only blackness, blankness.
Nice the mind is not racing.
Head on the pillow, maybe there will be rest.
No nightmarish visions. Quiet my mind.
Only see the blank expanse of space.
Would be nicer if I could imagine a sandy beach,
A meadow bursting with wildflowers, or a shimmering
blue light sky to drift and float in.
But not today—today it is only blank.

It is because I am sad.
It is an anniversary—3/9/99.
My father passed over into the nothingness.
Seven years have passed, the ache of grief gone.
Yet on this anniversary day: the body remembers.
There is a blackness behind my eyes.

The sadness is funny, it drips over shelves,
Like the timepieces in that Dali painting,
dripping and tripping down each step.
That is how sadness is, and it gets caught up in time,
it drips and floats and permeates the cells.
The sadness is referred to by body parts—
A broken heart, a tortured soul, soulful eyes, achy limbs,
crumbly bones, ashen complexion.
But let's not wallow in the sunken facial features.

Maybe there is hope. Visualize, change the blackness
into that blue sky, maybe put a few angels in it.
Let's romp through the lily fields or purple coneflowers,
And then the beach, my toes in the sand,
salt and sea spray on my face.

Ah mind, change my blood.
Visualize the peace and happiness of beautiful nature.
Hope it's as easy next time.

TODAY IS MY BIRTHDAY

This is a weird one.
By numbers, it's nothing important.
Somewhere in between fifty and sixty.
But by memory—"ah," another story.

All of a sudden, the mind is clear with memories
Of many other years.

I remember 10.
My father had a coupon for the Como Inn
He and I went there for dinner alone.
We were all dressed up.
It was my special time.
The musician waiters serenaded us.
I finished the meal with a cannoli.
I was in my father's fancy restaurant, cigar, music world.
Special.

Then Reza pops to mind.
The sweetest birthday man on the planet.
Not the richest, but the most giving—
A filigree mirrored perfume tray,
A plush Nordstrom robe,
when Chicagoans didn't even know from Nordstrom.
Never forgot.

But not the husband of fourteen years.
So unsure of himself. Couldn't surprise me.
Had to have me review beforehand.
Always sabotaging his own good deeds.
He's gone now—and probably
doing better birthdays for someone else.

There have been 14 birthdays since my daughter is in the world.
I have always felt lucky to be alive—because she is here.
I waited and wanted her so badly.
She always remembers. Always helps celebrate.
A pure Gemini—seeking to keep her Aries fiery mom happy.

Then the phone call yesterday from the first important love,
The one that got away. Just his voice, always, enough of a gift.
How does he know the right thing to say?
How can he be so strong?
How come he is not mine any longer?

I give up. Play the phone call sweet and light.
That's not what I am feeling.
Want to be Meredith to McDreamy.
Choose me, love me,
Doesn't matter—
almost thirty years since he walked away—
and on birthday day—
His voice made the difference.

Oh yeah the day is planned.
The friends have all come through.
I'm doing my yearly cosmetic makeover
Dinner at a fancy restaurant—just the girls.
My mom and my daughter.

They are both trying.
Give them an A for effort.

I guess we'll leave it at thank you
Spirit, G-d of the Universe, for another one.
As my friends say, "it's better than the alternative."

MY SAMANTHA

Sharon and Samantha.

WONDER BREAD

Early morning crispness,
no one on the roads, but
the moms and kids,
teenagers with their own cars,
and the delivery trucks.

"Oh look at that Wonder Bread truck!"
I exclaim to my seventeen year old
perfectly coiffed, lip gloss shining,
saucer round blue eyes glimmering.
"It reminds me of when we were kids,
look they have it painted like the fifties.
The Wonder Bread just the word—"WONDER"
in big beautiful red, and blue and yellow
circles like balloons."
Those were the primary color days.
The days of Twinkies and snowballs.
Simple Wonder Goodness, white bread.

"Yeah," my daughter says,
Now the upper classman stuff Twinkies in the freshman lockers.
"To do what?" I ask.
"So that when they open them,
Twinkies squish all over their books,
fall on them." Pranks.

Well not as bad to clean up as other things, I say.
Glad the Twinkies are stuffed in the lockers,
and not other orifices.
Food, Mothering, Wonder.
She is 17, but I see the two year old with three binkies,
one in the mouth, one in each hand.
Not even a Twinkie could have enticed away one of those plugs.

Hum, we settle back into our early morning bonding silence.
Nice to be up and out this early.
Even if I am with the rest of the stay at home moms—
lawyers, MBAs, accountants,
dropping the kids off at school in pajamas, under the coat.
The status symbol of the century,
have an advanced degree, a former profession,
and your husband makes enough money
for you to stay home with the kids and the nanny.

Wow another food truck. Doritos this time.
Not as nostalgic, but the whole side of the truck is
plastered with Doritos good enough to eat.

A-ha, after I drop off the beauty princess,
can I stuff the desire for the yellow arches?
Naw, not this morning.
Can't go into the bread place in pajamas.

We pull into the school line up.
She lumbers out, then stands up straight,
with a flick of the ponytail.
Already the new persona,
don't know who is watching.
Marches into the North Shore suburban white bread school.
I duck, want out of there, before I have to interact
and also juggle for position with these moms,
I left high school a long time ago.
On to the golden arches, to dream of Wonder Bread,
Egg McMuffins, Hohos, yum yum.
In the good ole Scarlett fashion, my errand for the day is done.
I'll think of the diet tomorrow.

Ah, the WONDER.

© Sharon D. Greenspan, 2010.

THE TERRIBLE TWELVES

Two was easy,
They had a temper tantrum,
You let them get over it,
Acted like it didn't happen.
Gave them choices,
"Do you want to wear the pink tutu
Or the purple mini skirt?"

Now it's not so easy.
Can't protect her from the class bully,
Or the joined at the hip snobs.
It's middle school, and it's all about
Fitting in . . .

But just where is that?

Misses the school bus,
The perfectionist; couldn't get everything in the bag,
One minute late, no one waits.

Drive her to the school
Have to put on my makeup,
Because if the mom's not cool,
Neither is the kid.

But I'm not cool.
I'm the oldest mom around, and I
Don't care.

I watch her tumble out of the car.
Watch the others as well.
Some walk upright, confident,
Swinging a glorious skirt, and ponytail
New puberty hips swaying as they go.

But most of them walk with heads down.
Books plastered against chests, so no
One sees the growth.
Can feel their pain.
Wonder if they will remember this time when they grow up.
She asks me all the time,
"How was middle school for you?"
Were the kids mean?
I have to tell her,
I honestly don't remember.
It obviously wasn't very traumatic for me.
However, I was in the city.
I was one of the smarter, richer kids in the neighborhood.
Didn't have much competition.

Had my few good friends.
Worried more about my parents fighting at home.
Loved books, school,
Didn't mind homework
Maybe for me it was a way out.

But for her, home
Even with its problems,
Is safer.

We talk.
I keep trying to give her my
Forty years of self-help, shrink, guru
Advice.

"Act like there isn't a problem."
"Don't take things personally."
"What goes around, comes around."
"It only takes one."

On good days, it works.
On bad days, she sluggishly saunters into school,
In her one pair of required 100 dollar Birkenstocks, head down,
Carrying her lunch, with half of it spilling out.

I drive away in the line,
Back home, and crawl under the covers.
Ah, good novel, take me away.

When she was two, three years old,
Used to sneak out, would have her involved in a game, or
video with the Nanny.

Didn't say goodbye, it created such a ruckus.
The crying; grabbing at my leg.
There was no explaining.
"I'm only going to the grocery store, the bank."
You know the song,
"My mommy comes back, she always comes back,
she never would forget me."

Now she's 12: went on a motor coach to overnight camp.
Someone sing, *"She always comes back,*
she always comes back,
My baby comes back, she never would forget me."

I look at the pictures on the camp website.
See how happy she is?
That's not what I see.
I see she's sitting alone too much.

In a week I've sent four packages, two letters, three e-mails.
We're symbiotically attached; she wakes in the night,
so do I—300 miles away.

I miss the softness of her cheek, a good night kiss.
Pre sleep whispers—
"How was your day, honey?" "Yours, mom?"

In her room I smell her pillow, kiss her pictures.
Try to get the grown-up things done,
But the space is too big; can't wait for her return.

VACATION WITH SAMANTHA

We looked out at the
beautiful ocean waves
From our balcony stateroom
The waters were blue
and frothy.
Sea spray almost to our faces.
Relaxation on our faces.

Brand new. Day one.
We are on a new adventure
Just the two of us.
We will make it if we can.
Just the two of us.
There is no love like this.

MUSINGS ON LIFE

COOKED CHICKENS

"My sister is dying, and I have to pick up the chickens!"
Barbara, fist clenched, my almost oldest friend, spit the words
into the phone.

"What do you mean, Barb?"

"They rushed my sister into ICU,
Her lungs filled up with toxic chemotherapy death.
They don't think she'll last the day."

"I have to make my kids dinner" (breathless)
"I have to pick up the chickens at Brooklyn Market,
Can you go for me?"

What is this about death, and
ordinary things?
We don't want to deal with death,
So we think about cooking dinner.

Barb is observant, her kids keep the *Sabbath*
They need a *Sabbath* meal their mother cooks,
Even though their aunt is dying? Is death a good spice?

"Barb, go to the hospital, don't worry about
the chickens," I plead softly.

"What will my kids eat?"

It is no use; it is a ruse.
She wants to know if I am there for her.
She does not want to talk, cry on my shoulder,
She wants me to pick up the chicken dinner.

I write down the number of the market.
I call. The chickens are not ready yet, call back later.
Maybe they're timing the death of the chickens,
With her sister.

Do chickens transition to the other side?
Do they go to heaven? Is the chicken dinner meant
to be her sister's first meal in heaven?
She's cooking for her sister, not her kids.

Our family has felt the swoosh of
that Angel of Death too many times in the past few years.

But in the past few months, she has passed over our house.
Each time I get a call, I breathe a sigh of relief.
Yes I will donate to a *Shiva* tray; yes I can make a funeral tomorrow,
Thank G-d, it is not us this time.

As my father lay in an ICU with tubes down him, trying to recover
from an open heart surgery, I sent my mother home with
my husband to rest.

I slept on a cold leather hospital smell couch, while my mother
nudged my spouse to take her to the jeweler to pick up her bracelets.

I screamed at her
"How can you think of jewelry, when
your husband is dying?!!!"

"Well, I took it there before we went to Florida,
And I don't know when I can pick it up"
Translation: nothing is happening here, if I put on my bracelets,
this bad dream will go away.

My anger overflowed, no one else wanted to save him,
She wanted to be bedecked for the *Shiva*.

My friend wants to cook dinner, so death will not be happening.
I will rearrange my day, pick up the chickens,
and wait for news of the funeral.
I am a good friend. I will cook a vegetarian dinner for my family.

PENNY KARMA

A penny glints in the concrete,
It beckons me to bend and snatch it up.
"Good Luck" penny.
There's another one, next to the construction worker's foot.
"Can you get it—It's Good Luck?"
His eyes scan me strangely; leans over and places it in my hand.
"Maybe it will bring YOU Good luck, Ha."

In this land of plenty—how have we become so jaded?
Rich twelve year olds in their *Rocketdogs, Abercrombie,*
Nike, and bling-bling have no use for pennies.

The infomercials tell us that 46 cents a day will feed
one starving child in Appalachia.
In Bangladesh, the pennies might buy a curry samosa.
In India, there are one million people who will be born,
live their whole life, and die on the street.
Can we shower them with pennies from heaven?

As for the Good Luck theory,
Here a penny, there a penny, everywhere a penny.
One penny can grow to ten.

A lucky penny, good karma, penny karma.

So—next time you see a penny—if you don't want or need it,
put it in the can of the Blind man/Veteran/Santa/Disabled person
standing on the corner with a can in his or her hand.

We can all make change, starting with a penny.

© Sharon D. Greenspan, 2000.

TIME . . .

I have come too far
    to listen to your voice—
Time . . .
I will accept your hands only as a caress,
    Not as a bludgeon.

I understand what few know
    You are
    Eternal
One can not stop you
You shall
Weave in and out of my past
    present and future life.

How man has tried to encase you
    to set you up by artificial names
    seconds, minutes, hours, days, months, years.

Must we always count?
    10 minutes till take off
    5 days till Christmas
    2 years till retirement
    6 weeks till delivery

Only those who understand your ebbs
    and flows and
    that we can't
    restrain you . . .
They live peaceably with you . . .

If not today, then
   tomorrow or the next day

Man's artificial clock shall not be
   my master

Your eternal unbridled rhythmic sway
   shall be my repose.

EXECUTIVE

Is he 'easygoing'?
Not 'too serious'
   is he?

Answers evade me.

At times,
   his face is a roadmap of obligations
torn and twisted by the should
   of a
   destructive culture.

Every line
   gained in worry,
a small victory of the punitive world.

Don't you understand?
There are no 'shoulds'
We are what
   we are, who
   we are.

Strong today
   weak tomorrow, sure now
   then confused
   brave, afraid.

We are a compilation
   of emotion
Don't restrain your inner self.

Just aspire to
   be human.

THE CHICAGO EL

And they piled on the train,
And rushed for their seats,
Knowing that standing would be a strain,
Whereas sitting was no great feat.

Before the conductors
could collect the extra fare,
It came billowing through the window,
Causing everyone a scare.

Where the hell did that come from?
Who could be so cruel,
Was it really a stone,
They just don't know the rules.

Is he hurt? I really don't know.
He's blinking his eyes in pain
And the blood is really beginning to show,
Get the conductor, stop the train!

"All right! All right!" the conductor exclaims
But first we must collect the fare from everyone on the train
It's really not that bad, it's a casual occurrence.
Anyone who's ever ridden this train, know it's not a first.

The fares are collected, the scare's forgotten,
The victim is rushed from the train,
And the passengers, pass off the incident as "rotten"
Saying such niceties as "Wasn't it a shame?"

But stay tuned folks, the time will come again.
When a rock will come crashing thru the trains
And who knows who fate has chosen for the victim,
Maybe next time you'll be the scapegoat, for Fate's whims.

LITTLE GIRL

It's 10 PM
At the corner of Diversey and Hampden Ct,
She walks into the bustling 7/11,
Her hair straggly.
Clothes a little dirty and unmatched.
As she lifts the can of Tab and can of orange soda
    onto the counter
The counter teen asks directly into
    her round blue eyes,
"It's a little past your bedtime,
    isn't it?"
She shakes her head,
    shuffles a little.
"Where's your mom and dad?"
"My mom's divorced," she explains.
"Oh, I see."
No further explanation necessary.

THE SECRETARY

I do not think, therefore I do not exist,
So it is little miss prissy secretary,
Type your type, correct your correction,
But do not think, for if you do,
You just may begin to exist,
Oh! Horrors of horrors, what
would you do with yourself if you were alive?

MOVING HOME

The rooms have changed,
All the clothes moved,
   and removed;
Furniture in storage.
I've returned to the nest.

They don't understand that my
   wings were clipped
   one time too many.
Became afraid to fly.
So I gave it up for Lent . . .

She rented my condominium,
   a younger me—
   looking for action.

Ah, the difference
   between 24 and 30.

And I return home.
Hoping to recapture my youth.

The scars from the scissors are
   permanent.
Fade creams, age creams work a little,
   but don't erase.

"Where do you live?," I'm asked.
"Well, it's a long story"
and they don't care to listen.

"You see, I just got old and tired,"
    had to give up the bubble baths and
    4:00 AM champagnes . . ."
They don't heal the scars.

Hope against hope,
    maybe mother's milk will.

SUNDAY AFTERNOON

Phone rings . . .
10:00 AM and the city is packing up
for brunch.

But,
it's the wrong caller.

"Sorry, I'm busy."
Roll over, try again.

11:00 AM.
"Hi,
Can I come up?"
She answers the door,
    torn robe, wet hair.
"Coffee's on . . ."

Conversation winds—
    this one wants commitment,
    that one can't handle it . . .

And Don McLean sings on.

"Winter has me at its grip . . ."
Restless wondering, years of analysis,
    questioning, understanding so much more
but yet not really changing—or really changing—
not quite sure.

The words sometimes spring,
and sometimes struggle,
and sometimes, there are none.

LIFE

There are many faces.
Happy and sad,
contemplative, sentimental,
Why are people all so
different?

They are all basically the same.

They have hunger, thirst, sex
sight, smell,
It's good that
different

    people mean

    different

    countenances.

How many faces
do you think you'll
see in the next sixty years

I want to see
millions of faces . . .

I thought of something funny today, as I went into my
Post Office (Deerfield, Illinois, that is.)

I was sending out bulk cards again, and I needed stamps.
But these were not happy cards.

These were thank you cards for all of the expressions of sympathy,
for the passing of my mom, Sylvia Greenspan, on 08/05/08.
I knew the clerk,
because I had bought large quantities of stamps from her for
My wedding invitations 1991.
Birth announcements of Samantha, 1992.
At least 12 birthday parties, Samantha 1993—thru 2005.
Three graduation parties for Shoshana,
middle school—1992, high school—1996, and college—2000.
Sylvia and Phil's 45th wedding anniversary party, 1991.
Thank you notes for expressions of sympathy
when Phil passed, 1999.
Sylvia's 80th birthday party, 2000.
Samantha's *Bat Mitzvah,* November 2005.
. . . and all of those thank you notes; all of those invitations.

Is it true you can tell who someone is by their mail?
Like on the cop shows when they look for clues.

By this time I felt a sense of history.
I was glad we had lived in the same town for 16 years.
I was glad the post office clerk had been there when I was crying
and sending off a package to Samantha at camp,
while my mother was dying in the ICU.

Who is it who listens to us? Our friends get tired.
But those not-so-strange strangers, they know.
The post office clerk who has handled your mail for years knows.
Of course the hair dresser listens,
and the lady at the dry cleaners,
and the clerk at the fast food drive-in know you.

You see my mom is gone. My world has changed.
It is good to know that others have noticed.

I AM OLD AND I AM NOT WEARING PURPLE

I am old, and I am not wearing purple.
I am wearing red; it is Valentine's Day.
I am alone, but I put on a fancy red sexy top
and went to . . .
where?
First, acupuncture.
Clothes come off.
Not for a man.
For tiny hair thin needles up and down this old body.
Restore my qi energy.
As I lay on the massage table, my senses are heightened.

I remember briefly other Valentine's Days,
I was worried "What would he buy me?
Chocolate, Flowers, Jewelry?
Was always testing them.
Maybe that is why I am alone now.
But I don't need to wallow in it.
I'm still here.
I still have a red blouse.
Session is over.
Needles removed.
Slight massage.
Put my red blouse back on.

Joke with happily married acupuncturist.
She's got new house this year, so no chocolates.
I sent gifts to my lovechild.
I shall wear red and treat myself to a simple Chinese buffet.
I don't have to come home and "look at the four walls"

So I now sit in my red blouse,
sipping on wonton soup
and listening to a Tony Bennett CD, in a high end China Bistro.
Tony Bennett is 84, and singing with the women.
Winehouse, Liza, Celine, who else?

I am old and I am wearing red . . .
Smack, smack
Kisses, yum
Love me.

I HATE TUESDAYS AT 10:30 AM

I hate Tuesdays at 10:30 AM
They interrupt my TV,
Beep, beep, beep
"This is the required emergency
broadcast test."
I am so calm.
Then those pretend air raid sounds.
Hackles up my back.
If I were a terrorist, I would plan an attack on Tuesday morning—
10:30 AM.
It is like the boy who cried wolf—too many times
It's Tuesday at 10:30 AM.
It's only a test.
This is a test of the emergency broadcast system.

Fear, fear, fear
I guess love really is letting go of fear
This is just a test . . .

Devastating—I have gotten old—
And wearing purple does not matter.
My 92 year old friend Helen laments that she has no one
All her friends are dead.
She is all alone.
Yet she refuses to go to one of those communal places—deep down
It must remind her of the camps.

I am 62. Will turn 63. No big parties thrown for me anymore.
My daughter is twenty—she had twenty phenomenal birthday celebrations.
I now have to find someone to grace my presence.
My older friend laments—was I a bad mother?
Why does my son visit only every few months?
And my daughter, once a week,
but with duty—runs out of here as quickly as possible.

I have a different problem.
The few friends I have left call me
for advice with their problems.
When I am really sad—no one to call.

They don't want to hear it.
The pain in my body and soul are unbearable—
the loss of who I am unbearable—
if I cry I am told I'm just trying to get attention.
If I voice my ideations that I would rather die—
they think it is for affect.
'You always say that—you will never do it.'

Had an MRI. White spots on my brain—
neurologist believes it is cardiovascular, not neurological.
So when tingling runs down my right side—
maybe take another blood pressure pill.
Yeah, fight with insurance to get another blood pressure pill.

Why go on?
I guess my daughter would be hurt—
but maybe better off?
No longer any push or pull—
her dad would be happy to have her to himself.
Her sister would be jealous to share her.
I see no purpose.

There is a void.
When Helen used the terms "I look at four walls"—
I was the cheerleader.
Read books, watch new television programs,
I've watched every episode of *Pawn Stars* and *Storage Wars*.
I look at four walls.

So like the pope—time to resign.
I resigned from work due to illness twenty years ago.
Now I will resign myself to words.
I still have my words, my memories,
occasional encouragement from friends.
And that's what saves me.

WHEEL IS MY SAVIOR

Round and round and round she goes,
Where she stops, nobody knows.

Wheel of Fortune, saved my day
Wheel of Fortune, take me away.

America's savior throughout the land,
everyday same time, same brand.
In nursing homes across the country
after dinner it's Wheel Time, honey.

And why is it America's favorite game show?
Throughout the world, actually,
Because on Wheel of Fortune, everyone wins.

Big, small, fat, skinny, brown, black, yellow, red, white,
all across America, everyone wins.

If you lose, you go home with $1,000.
If the Wheel lands on bankrupt, you get another chance.
There are trips to foreign places
and cars in half and half on different spaces.
And smiling faces, and simple solves.

Vanna, now just touches and lights up the screen
We love her for her beauty, timelessness, sweetness, never a scowl.
And Pat, well what can you say to good ole Say-Jack?
Yakshemash?
He's a Chicago boy made good.
He clicked his heels and stayed right with that Wheel
All this time.

No matter how bad the day, no matter how much pain
Wheel is there to make it alright.

May I live to watch Wheel with my grandchildren
as they learn their letters.
"Grandma, what's that spell?"
Love, love, love . . .
Spin the wheel.

OUT OF THE RUBBLE: *CFIDS AND THE WTC*

We, the longtime survivors
Of this horrible plague
Watched the towers go up in smoke,
With mixed emotions.
(Suddenly the world is upside down)

On the one hand,
How could things get any worse?
We had been devastated for so long by CFIDs
But many times there was comfort in knowing our country was well.
We could rely on its resources.

But yet at the same time,
A shameful feeling,
Watching all the mourners,
The commentators, the services—
One thought "a-ha!"
Maybe they now will understand what we have gone through . . .

How it hit us like lightning?
How we weren't sure if it was an accident
Or intentional? Why me?
How some of us managed to escape with only minor injuries
Then got on with our lives
(Those so-called PWCs who have recovered)

How some of us have been changed forever
Now maybe the world will listen.
I do believe you have to experience pain to be sensitive to it.

Obviously, Bin Laden's fanatics with their holy *Jihad* thought so.
They hurt—so they will make us hurt.
And now the cycle will continue.

Then we also watched feeling helpless.
We can't donate blood—ours isn't any good.

We aren't physically able to dig through the rubble
We can barely take care of ourselves—how can we help?

Then it comes slowly,
We know all about attacks,
And the grieving process.
Maybe we can help our nation through this grief—
As only those who have lost before know how.

WHAT KIND OF DAY IS TODAY? (AN ODE TO CFIDS)

Is today a day where I can lift my head?
Or is today a day where I can lift a pot to cook?
Is today a day of Wheel of Fortune?
Or is today a day of writing a novel?
Or maybe just settling for reading a novel.

How does one keep up your spirits?
The body aches, the brain fog settles over.
Only able to unload half a dishwasher,
Pretty much consigned to the bed
Now with an iPhone, the world is your oyster—from bed.

Except your arm hurts from typing,
Your eyes water at the screen,
You try and journal, but what to say?
Thank G-d I'm not dead.
Thank G-d I can still afford groceries, maybe.

Try and make phone friends with the elderly.
Those in their eighties and nineties.
If they're not sick—they don't get it.
How to not be a malingering piece of crap
when all you have is an illness that lingers.

It comes back to what kind of day?
Too many days with no improvement,
And the mind turns to hurtful things,
Fall down the rabbit hole.

After I dry my tears, I turn to my voices of inspiration:
G-d, Jewish singers, Louise Haye,
Rabbi Eitan, Joel Osteen, Mark Nepo.
Today, someone give me the word.
All clear. You are healed!

ON JUDAISM AND SPIRITUALITY

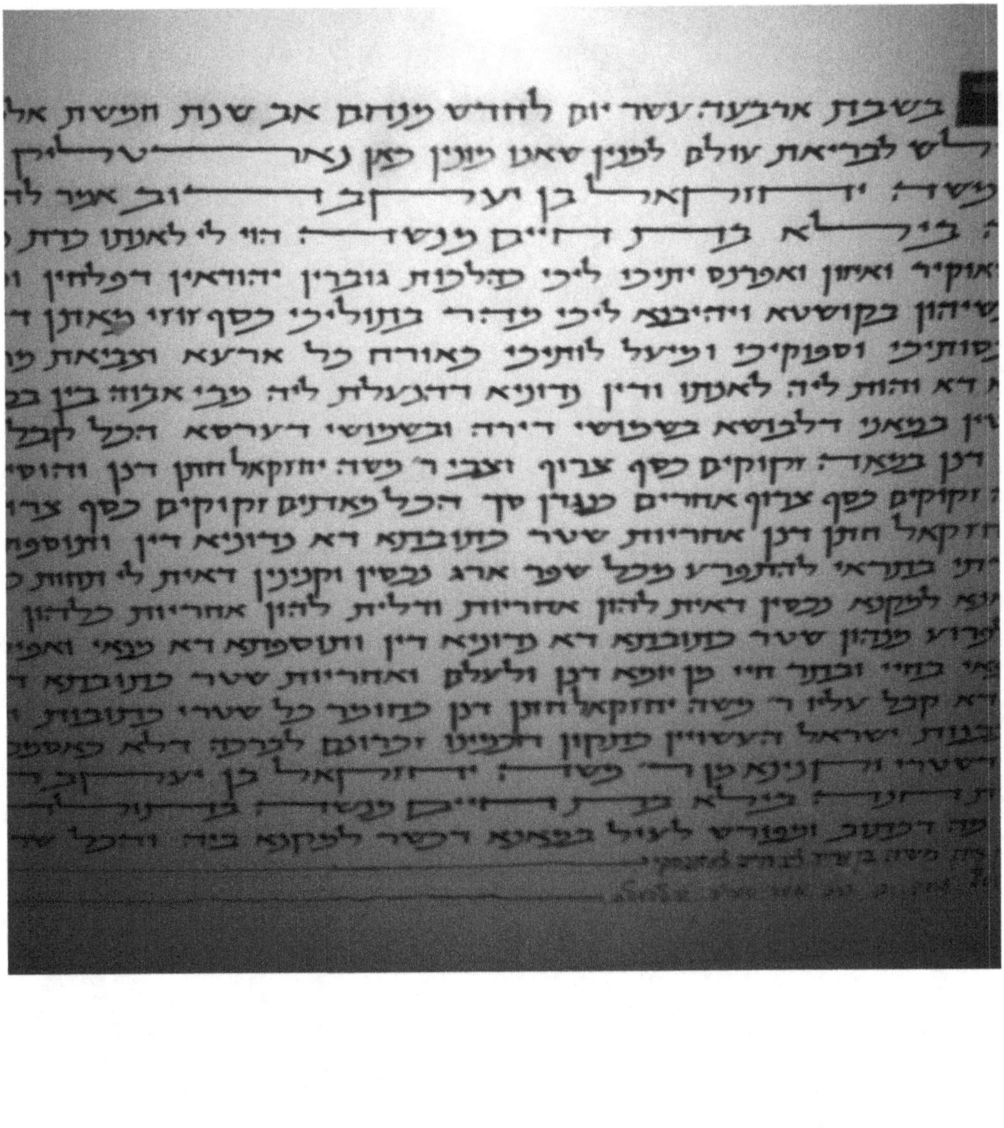

AVODAH

AVODAH,
Work in an ancient language,
Work translated . . .
    to stand . . .
Ah, but why?
    We no longer stand in holiness.

ARBEIT MACHT FREI
These words
    the symbol of the myth
    we bought
    to destroy us, and
    even in freedom we still
    let it destroy us.

Like a hamster in a cage,
    we run
    spinning the wheel
    only to return
    to the same place.

If you worship
    false gods
They shall forsake you.

The Golden Calf is
    easily shattered.

Worship the wonders of creation,
   not the false idols of man.

Work does not
   make you free,
Only freedom
   makes us work.

THE PLAGUES OF PESACH

So our ancestors were slaves in Egypt,
And now sometimes I feel that we are slaves too.
Why do we Jews always have to dwell on the suffering?
Are we supposed to break our backs,
and cry as we grate the *marror*?
Cleaning cabinets, and shelving paper,
and bringing up the boxes.
Don't we suffer enough?

As a kid I loved it.
I remember those Seders at Bubbe Helen and Zayde Moshe's house.
Got to sit at the end of the table and drink from the barrel glasses.
Happy that it caused us to come together at least once a year.
Happy that we had 30 people in our family to put around a table.

Everyone complained because Fischel, my dad, didn't smile.
He hated *Pesach*, as do I. He worked so hard.
I guess that's what it's about,
passing down a heritage to our kids—
The one year we did it at my house with him,
I had a compatriot. He was as organized as I.
It's kind of like the worker bees,
and the ones who enjoy the honey.

Pesach is about hope and joy. Hope with Elijah's cup.
Samantha loves Pesach because she feels
at that time of the year like she has a big family.
Samantha will always remember the Seders
at Bubbe Sylvia and Zayde Fischel Greenspan's house.

Let us enjoy the telling of the story—of how G-d
with an outstretched arm took us out of Egypt.
Let us think of the 2,000 years of Jews all over the world,
who are doing the same thing as we—
and somehow know—that to do this is holy.

So even though my legs ache, and I'm exhausted
from the cleaning and the shopping, and the lining the shelves,
and cleaning the ovens,
I shall smile—
to see my lovely nieces and nephews,
my wonderful aunts, uncles and cousins—
and our by now related family (all the *machetanim*).

Blessed is the Lord our G-d who brought me to see this day.
Shalom chaverim. L'Chaim to one more *Pesach.*
So let's please try and do it in peace.

FOR ISRAEL

In the year 1948
this nation became a state.
Her people work hard and toiled
To raise crops from barren soil.

But the neighbors on all sides,
They raised their sticks and cried:
You cannot be free,
For you took that land from me.

But who will pay the price?

So their neighbors waged war,
The dove was wounded and sore
They raised their voices endlessly
"We will push you into the sea"

The name of the game was chess
And everyone wanted their chance
to see who could be the best:
Russia, The USA, or France.

But the world will never understand,
That we will never leave our land.
For once in the world we can be free,
To live in our very own country.

THE WORLD TRADE CENTER:
TOWER OF BABEL

"Bismillah-ir-Rahman-ir-Rahim"
"Shema Yisrael Adoshem Echod"
Our father who art in heaven—hallowed be thy name.

Were we praying in too many languages?
Were the towers too big?
What right did they have to soar to the heavens?
Did G-d smash them as the Golden Calf?

Is Bin Laden a prophet to turn us
away from the money-making, idolatrous society we have created?

Sad to believe that could be the point of such destruction.
There is no why or wherefore—no sense in madness.

Erev Rosh Hashanah.

HONORING FRIENDS
AND FAMILY

Sylvia Haberman Greenspan, and her seven grandchildren.

BRUNCH

Every so often we realize,
That our friends are what make our lives full.
But yet each one seems to carry a separate part of us,
And we, a separate part of them.

So in an effort of unity,
I wish for all my favorite friends
To meet each other
So that the circle
Can be completed . . .

In honor of my favorite friends:
Brunch.

FOR TRACY, ON HER BIRTHDAY

I come today bearing no gifts,
No fig spread, brie cheese,
curries or hummus spread.

Today I come only with the gift of words.
It is a belated birthday wish to Tracy
The friend of all friends.

She wonders why we all love her,
Why we flock to her, why we all want to be her friend?
Who wouldn't want a friend who is so non-judgmental,
So loving, so always there with an ear,
So always striving for the higher road.

She thinks she doesn't have that many friends,
Ah—but her modesty is just one of her additional traits.
Walk in a room with Tracy, and see the butterflies swirl.
They all want to be next to that goodness, sweetness kindness,
Hope maybe it will rub off.

Or better yet that oh so deserved good karma.
Love how she hates those whining women characters in any
of the book club selections.

"I couldn't stand her!" "She cared only for herself."
And her favorite book, Truth and Beauty,
about a friendship of two authors,
one who was facially deformed by cancer and multiple surgeries—
and the other?
With a heart as big as the Iowa farmland.

You know which one is our Tracy.
Heart as big as the State.

So my gifts to you are—cherish who you are—
This birthday year.
We all cherish you.

FOR TAMAR

Oh, Tamar, Tamar, Tamar,
She looked near and far
All throughout the Kingdom
To find a man worthy of her fiefdom

Then came Trevor with his wafting lilt,
And he sure gave Tamar's head a tilt.
He courted her from land to sea,
and soon they—became a we.

The news rang out throughout the land.
Trevor had asked for Tamar's hand.
With the blessed nuptials soon approaching,
We thought perhaps Tamar needed a little coaching.

So from your friends gathered here today,
This is what we have to say.
Although it sounds funny, trite and true,
To each other always be true blue.

Never go to bed mad.
Try not to make each other sad.
Bring laughter and cheer to your home,
May your love make all feel welcome.

Love each other with all your might,
Do all things necessary to make it right,
May the road be long and happy,
For this lovely lad and lassie.

Love and kisses from us all.
A toast to Tamar, the fairest bride of the fall.

RUTH ANNE

True Friends,
Best Friends,
How do we count the time?
The years gone by, the years yet to experience.
Shared times, hopes, dreams, tears.

My friend,
true blue, generous, giving, loyal to a fault.
Strong when I was weak.
Yet thankfully, sometimes—
weak when I was strong.

Balance,
It is the "time you have wasted on your
rose that makes her so important," thus
sayeth the Little Prince through the
eyes in his heart.

You have
watered many a garden and sewn many seeds.
Let us celebrate . . .
Yet this additional rite of passage.
You have arrived . . .
You have achieved.
You're great . . . and I'm glad
to be part of your magical
circle of friends.
Happy Birthday!

© Sharon D. Greenspan, 1988.

THE THIRTEENTH TALE

And so our book club tells the story.
The Thirteenth Tale. A magical time
Filled with birth, death, deceit, cruelty and love.
Read as a mirror to those things in all of our lives.
NUMBERS—buried my mom on 08/08/08
Aurelius in the novel, received a birthday and news of his mother's death,
at the same time.
Our names, our outward incantations, of our ancestors and their
hopes for the future.
The cycles come and go with this book.

The group comes together for The Thirteenth Tale.
We have been together for a while.
We each bring different pieces to this story.
We are creating a story that so far has no name.

What shall we call it? Will the survivors find bits and pieces to try
and put together a name? The letters tumble, T, B, MMM, E, C, P, S & S.
A tea cup—tea for Tamar, Theresa, or ah, Tracy—or Truth, Truth Tracy
lights the way—brings us to the truth of ourselves, our books, our tales.
Sing thy praises loud and clear.

Half an English biscuit, bat of mercy, Bata, or Betty—or Beth—as in the
sturdiness of the *Beth Din*. The house that is strong even in the desert.
The shelter that is needed from the storm. The structure that is needed
above the chaos.

T & B—ah, there is an M—no, two Ms—no, three Ms, a pack of M&Ms!
We have found half a biscuit, a tea cup and a pack of M&Ms.
There is the perfectly shaped M that quietly takes her place in the package.
Not pushing anyone aside, but holding her ground, strength when all others
are weak—that M is not mushy, or marshy—but her mysteries and depth of

feeling run deep—so we shall let her be like the marshes—
mysterious, but beautiful and deep—Marsha.

Then there is another M—bright red, smiling, and putting a
band aid on any child's knee. Aunt to us all. Shiny as an oyster,
a real pearl, with bright inquisitive eyes, that Aunt Merle.
Bringing us back from melancholy when necessary.

The third M—does not always speak her name—she joined us
in spirit later—she has flash, flare and a bit of the French,
but she brings the European roots to the table—ah, Mimi,—
mum's the word—Mimi, mmmmmm.
We need a vowel. I'll buy an E. But this E cannot be bought.
This E is eternal, ethereal and editorial when needed. She is the elder—
our sage speaks—forcefully and brilliantly. Eileen props
us all up with her wisdom and experience.

Wait, there are more, the P and the C—swirling with the E.
But each a letter unto themselves. Are they the cornerstones?
We have read of fires, cinders, and caring. We have traveled to China,
Crimea, cold war Russia, Cuba and the Caribbean—Cindy has laid the
terrain—asked the different questions, brought the different perspective.
Caring while being caustic or critical. Cementing us when necessary.

The P. Ah, P for purity and the pope, and a purpose-driven life.
Purity in its highest form. Have we reached nirvana? One of us is close.
Peering from those perfect peaceful eyes—but petulant as well.
One can never get one's fill of Phyllis.

PEC—Is that a word? If we put an S at the end, we have PECS. We pec
each other on the cheek in greeting. If we put another S at the front we have
SPECS—glasses, mirrors, tiny traces, specs of each of us in each other.

One S, is for the mother to us all. She is a mother who can support, yet keep
a secret. See, but not squeal. Support, but not suffocate. Earth mother with
class. Never late, never lost, a beacon in the night—that is our Sally light.
Leading with laughter all the way . . .

The other S is a shadow to us all. Sure but not. Sweet but not.
Is there a sugar cube next to those M&Ms? Soulful and soothing.
But sharp and at times, sarcastic, sinister.

She does seek to share though, and that is her salvation.
So Shar comes out of the shadows for a moment.

And so the Shadow seeks to reveal all of us through The Thirteenth Tale.
We have arrived. We have come to the end of the story.
There are letters that join us from time to time—but they have to stay
longer to find a place in the story.

So this time the story is dedicated to us. We are The Thirteenth Tale.
We all have our stories. We have brought them to each other, through the
magic of books and the holy words of our authors. Some day in the future—
someone will find our bits and pieces and try and make sense of this tale.
S's for stories—spirits that are here.

But lest The Thirteenth Tale be a golden calf, we shall add a G—for grace
and goodness and G-d. For in the end, G-d is with me and I shall not fear.
Now to the next story.

In honor of our Riverwoods, Illinois, book club, "Tracy's Girls".

AN ODE TO CAROLE-TOWNE

Caroling, caroling through the woods,
With my friend Carole Kaye Good.
Does she sing, this Carol bird?
No she chirps and flies on Towne-ship wings—
She flaps her feathers and soars,
Bringing love and calm to all shores.

Caroling merrily through the town—turning frowns upside down.
She's my friend from way, way back
Because she's always softly had my back . . .
Her Care-Role is that, she's a flapjack, best tack, best friend in Towne.
She'll never let you down;
Raised on loyalty, brains and good looks,
There is nothing else like her in The Book.

She once said, with raised glass, as I was taking leave.
"Here's to ten great years" in the Chicago land of Towne.
But, I journeyed on and found—there was no greater land than
Carole-Towne.

It is now 30 years later and I say to the precious Carole Kaye—
Here's to thirty more—so someone can say
"Where or where in this fair land is the best place to buy radials?*
Now lesser men won't understand this reference.
Scaling in the brine, maybe Scalambrino knows the secret reference to tires
in the land.

Carole keeps a hidden truth—we won't need to buy radials. *
We'll just click our heels and fly, because our home was there all the time.
Caroling, caroling thru the woods . . .
Happy Mother's Day Carole Kaye Good.

*This is a private joke: Carole always remembered my parents arguing in strong Yiddish accents, as to whether or not my mother's car needed tires, or really whether to spend the money.

JEFF GUSFIELD'S BAR MITZVAH

May your voice soar with the
help of the souls of your ancestors,
May you stand in the thousand year line
that has stood before you.
May your heart be glad, your family
rejoice, and your community be proud.
May G-d shine his countenance down on you
and say
"This is good."

Congratulations! May we all share in your
blessings and jubilation.
Mazel Tov!

MY UNCLE JACK

Do you have an Uncle Jack?
Everyone should have an Uncle Jack.
My friends all ask "How's Uncle Jack?
That's pretty impressive as we're all turning 60.

My Uncle Jack, Cracker Jack, Wonder Jack, Magic Jack
probably even lumberjack.
No task was ever too big for my Uncle Jack.

Cause my Uncle Jack was big, big, big.
When I was a little girl,
I would run to him and he would lift me up high.
My Uncle Jack would have surprise candy
in his White Hardware shirt pocket.
Such sweetness. He loved us all. His heart was as big as he.
When I was a big girl, I could run to him with my problems,
and he was still, big, big, big.
Always an answer. Always build you up.

Memories I have of getting on a plane to Boston
to save my brother Jay (or so we thought that was the mission).
My Uncle Jack and Aunt Judy with me at the airport.
My Uncle Jack stuffing me with money,
Aunt Judy instructing where to put it.
He was always larger than life, big with life's big problems
as well as a smile with the small ones.

I remember my *Zayde* in a hospital bed.
Speaking in Yiddish. Crying as dying.
But he said to my aunt, "There is no one like Jack.
When they made Jack they threw away the pattern."
Threw away the pattern . . . an original.

All of us scruffy Greenspan/Marshak nieces and nephews grew up—
and Uncle Jack was still there.
"Uncle Jack can you get me a faucet for my bathroom?"
"Uncle Jack I'm having this business problem, what should I do?"

But he also made us feel good about our achievements,
relying on our expertise.
The lawyers doing the lawyering,
the daughters doing the doctoring, ministering, cooking.
The business guys and gals helping with the business plan.

We all loved the most loveable Uncle Jack.
He taught us all what love is.

Love is patience, love is going on even when it is difficult,
love is overcoming grief and loss,
love is abundant joy in the miracle of birth,
in the solemnity of religious observance and *simchas*.
He never missed a *simcha* if he could help it.

Best of all, love is a good joke.
How many of us can remember Uncle Jack saying:
"Did you hear the one about . . . ?"

We all want to be here to celebrate his 100th.
My heart is filled with love for my Uncle Jack.
My daughter Samantha loves my Uncle Jack as her own.

The rabbi, priest and minister will all walk on water,
like in the joke, or be at the shoreline,
drink in hand, mariachi band in the background to celebrate.
Or maybe we'll rent out Ruby Foo's in Montreal to party.

So let's celebrate the 90th. Okay guys, drink in hand,
salsa band in the background,
G-d's shining face smiling down on Uncle Jack,
and all of us blessed to know and love him.
L'chaim.

Uncle Jack passed away at the age of 91, a year later.

TEN AUNTS AND UNCLES

Ten aunts and uncles
ten fingers and toes
Those ten loved each other and loved us.

Immigrants in the fifties
overcoming the memories of World War II,
My dad, Phil, had two
My mom, Sylvia, had three
All of my five aunts and uncles married other people
Five times two equals ten.

Sterling and Freda, a true *bashert*
Mom's baby brother, the character.
At thirteen, with Hitler looming,
he came to his mother in Vienna and said
"Sign this paper—
I'm going on a kinder transport."
He went to Canada, by way of England
All alone at thirteen.
Sterling and Freda, always good for a laugh
fun, but could be relied on in a pinch
He saved her life, a stroke at the age of 38
She loved him forever.

Then Irving and Francis, see how they rhyme?
Sterling and Freda, Irving and Francis . . .
They were the Chicago couple, like my folks
solid, hardworking, North siders.
Always in apartments in Rogers Park.

My sweet sixteen—my Aunt Francis
gave me an onyx ring with a diamond in the center.
She gave a speech, and she was not a public speaker.
"This is a ring passed to me from my aunt.
I am passing it to you as my niece.
This ring is meant to go from aunt to niece."
I wore that ring all through college,
and into adulthood.
I passed it to my niece, Eva, on her Bat Mitzvah.

Then also on mom's side, there was Leah and Max,
Leah, the oldest, the strongest, the true survivor
Tante Leah, the arranged marriage in Europe yet.
Leah's progeny are three children, over fourteen grandchildren
and too many great grandchildren to count.
What a legacy . . .
It takes numbers to survive.
Ten aunts and uncles.

Then, the Greenspan side.
Judy and Hoskel, the beatnik lovebirds.
He, the intellectual, no one thought he would marry.
It was the fifties, he worked at a national laboratory.
He had a Ph.D. in mathematics,
but he found his intellectual equal.
My aunt Judy. University of Chicago, all the way.
Her own person.
My wonderful mentor in the early lawyering days.
She knew how to be a professional woman.

Lastly, Dorothy and Jack.
Oh, my auntie Dorothy.
They always said I looked like her.
I loved her deeply.

Her and my mom were the cooks, the *Yiddishe mamas*
but they both had heads for business,
Boy could they get you a deal.
And Dorothy had the best, Jack,
Cracker Jack, my uncle Jack, one of the magnificent ten.

Ah, that we could package ten aunts and uncles;
Patent it, promote it, sell it on QVC.
Ron Popeil, move over.

TANTE LEAH

Tante Leah,
She was the strong one.
The eldest of four;
All of the responsibility on her shoulders
And she carried it well

How can we possibly understand what those
War years were like?
Entrusting your two baby boys to French Nuns
For awhile, or forever.
Watching people shot in the street.

In later years, Alzheimer's can be its own blessing.

There were the good times.
Uncle Max, her scholar.
Traipsing Sylvia throughout Europe in search of a *shidduch*.
Later going back to Vienna for the cures.

Sylvia found her Raffi on her own.
Aunt Leah knew what a gem they had found in him.

Her sons did a great job, too.
It is a true accomplishment, 90,
Nine grandchildren, eighteen great grandchildren.
A matriarch all the way.
Yet she and *Hashem* chose her time.
She took her time.

One strong memory of my aunt and I alone is etched in my mind.
Just she and I.
I took a train trip back from Chicago to New York with her
I had never been in a sleeper car.
I had never been in a dining car.
I loved that train, and that trip.
She was a woman whom when she spoke, you listened.

She has gone and joined her husband, parents and brothers.
I'm sure she's back in charge.
Magnified and sanctified be thy name, O lord our G-d.

© Sharon D. Greenspan, 2004, *on the passing of Leah Haberman Zavderer.*

THOSE TWO GUYS

I think of them often,
One the Peacemaker,
the other a bit of a Troublemaker.
In life thrown together when
their kids got together.
Now they are up in heaven together.

Eddie I didn't know as long—but
He had a great way of cutting to the chase.
Some of his favorites:
If you don't have anything good to say, don't say anything.

He thought his kids were the best in the world.
His family was the best, and when you were with him
that's how you felt.
Phil, larger than life, Dancing, Tennis,
and hot Polish like Latin blood.
But Integrity. Always said what was on his mind.
Didn't know how to tell a lie.
They were our respective families' rocks.
Both Soldiers who fought in the War to end all Wars.
One in Europe and One in the Pacific.
Both saw horrors no one could speak of.
Both honored with medals.

There is no coincidence that they died one year apart.
Their *Yahrzeits* in the Jewish calendar are almost the same.
Eddie had his nicknames for everyone.
"SammiBelle"—No one else could call Samantha that name.
Like a football jersey, since he has been gone—
that name has been retired.

And *Zayde* Greenspan—dancing,
Samantha will always remember being six years old,
And being allowed into a nightclub downtown—
to dance with *Zayde*.
Like a scene right out of the movie <u>The Five Little Pennies</u>.

She has inherited well from both of them.
She is a peacemaker, doesn't gossip,
always tells it like it is, and is a great dancer.
They are watching from Heaven. Commenting, joking.
They are here today in Spirit.
We wish they were here in the Flesh.
She, their joint granddaughter has made us all proud.
Let us remember them and honor the legacy they left us.
Osay shalom bim romav.
Who Ya'aseh Shalom Aleinu,
V'al Kol Yisrael V'Imru—Amen.

FOR ALEX KULIK

"The good die young."
We hear this expression all the time
But what does it mean
And how often does it really apply?

To Alex, it is the entire expression
Of his passing.
It is the expression of the dignity with
which he and his family handled the past few months.
He was told in February that there was
a combatant growing within him.
His goodness and intelligence made him want to fight.
He fought the glorious fight.
In his own way. Lots of people did not agree
with his desire to go to Europe for treatment.
But he had to follow his own heart.
Unfortunately, the young guardians
of our traditional medical teams,
did not give him enough hope.
So he went toward the hope.

Alex had that strong immigrant will, determination and caring.
He was all goodness.
What does that mean?
It means that he would give you the shirt off his back.
If he saw someone in distress he was the first to give a hand out.
He was all empathy—he exuded it.
Sometimes when someone gives to the whole world,
it can be hard on his immediate family.
You wonder if there is enough for you.
But there is. Because when you have a heart of gold,
it is the largest most welcoming room in the world.
There is always room at the inn with someone of a heart of gold.

We will all remember his smile, his strong opinions,
always looking for a good political argument.
His great wit. Always wanting the stimulation of being alive.

That is why he chose to go as he did.
He didn't want to lose his hair.
He didn't want to put additional poisons in his body.
He fought the cancer, but at a certain point
he decided that a peaceful retreat was the best way to go.

He did just that. He went with dignity.
With a loving family, his brother, mother
and wife all around his bedside.
Everyone putting aside their differences to love Alex,
who brought them all together in the first place.

For Gary, Melissa and Sara, you must know in your heart
that you have just got yourself a guardian angel.
He will always be there for you when you need him.
You will always carry him in your heart,
right next to G-d, where he is now.

We are all just souls who inhabit a material body for a while.
When we go, we go to all goodness.
That is where Alex is now,
and he will always be there for you.

When this time of pain and grief passes,
you will remember all the good times.
The trips to Lake Geneva, to Florida, summers in the backyard,
at pools, the 4th of July—and his great barbecue.

Alex and Eva and the kids were truly inspired and moved
by the compassion, generosity and love of the entire church,
school and Winnetka community these past few months.
The nightly dinners really do make a difference
when you go through something like this.

It helps to make one feel protected,
to move away from fear and into love.
The whole Kulik family can never thank you enough.
They have seen how the world can be a loving place,
and hope that support will continue through their grief and transition.

The rest of us were honored that Alex graced our lives.
Not for long enough, but obviously
G-d felt his work here was done in the flesh.
He will now do his work in the spirit
and continue to inspire us all.
Alex is the meaning of only the good die young.
We will miss him, but he will live on in our hearts.

N'SHAMA CHAYA, FOR BETTY KOGAN

When we leave this Earth,
We hope we have lived *good,* have been *good,*
so that our souls transmigrate ahead,
to a wondrous place.

Or we come back for another try at perfection.
Betty Balter Kogan had a true *n'shama chaya.*
Her soul shall move forward, since she was the essence
of goodness. She doesn't need another go 'round.

So many strive to be above it,
to take the high road,
to not engage in small talk, gossip, *lashon hara.*
Not all achieve this.

She achieved this in everything she did.
The stories of her and Abe filled my childhood.
There is no one both of my parents looked up to more.
They were so different than my parents,
yet there was an affinity.

How can you describe what closeness is?
Some 64 years ago my mother got married to Phil
in Betty's wedding dress.
Months before my father was best man at
Abe and Betty's wedding.
My mother held up the start of the wedding,
she was *shomer Shabbos.*
Two years ago, my mother and a helper drove through floods
to be at their home for a break fast on Yom Kippur.

I remembered them always being there for us.
Betty was there for us at B'nai Emunah.
We the kids didn't all know each other that well,
but we sure knew each other's parents.

I am sorry I did not spend more time with her this year.
I know that she is a *n'shama chaya*.
A soul in the beyond—hanging out with the rest of
them. I am sure the Balters were there to greet her.

The most important legacy you can leave your children,
your community, is to live an upstanding, generous yet humble, right life.
This Betty did. This is her legacy.
All who knew her will miss her.

For Abe, let our love envelop you at this time, as she did her whole life.

L'vorrechecha v'yeeshmarecha, cain yehi ratzon.

IN HONOR OF WILLIAM B. ODENCRANTZ

Bill, my days with you,
although they were 30 years ago
are as vivid as yesterday.

I felt so honored to be in a new job.
Assistant Regional Counsel,
Immigration and Naturalization Service,
San Pedro, California.
I sat across from you,
your big government desk
with piles on each side.
But you knew what was in the piles.

Everyone was scared of you.
You were young.
In your thirties, but silver hair.
A case of hepatitis you explained:
in your 20s, turned your hair white.
But you were a clear stand-in
for Doogie Howser, M.D.
only it was William B. Odencrantz, J.D.
(Bolt Hall, no less)
If you didn't have the
white hair—they'd think you
were fifteen.

Until you spoke;
Then it was like listening
to geniuses on Jeopardy.
The Immigration Gods in Washington D.C.
thought you would do

better with a woman Assistant Regional Counsel,
than the few guys who had
tried before me.
It wasn't a sexist thing.
They knew you listened
to your strong, professional
wife Donna at home.
So maybe it would work at the office.

Everyone was scared or bewildered by you.
Your military training
showed its head many a time.

Your authority was wonderful
for the Chief Border Patrol agents,
and the Regional Commissioner,
and the heads of deportation, and investigation.

But the direct line attorneys
who you direct line supervised
sometimes there was dissension—
as is common with us lawyers.
A quiet lawyer generally doesn't fare so well.

So I looked at you across the desk,
listened to the horns of the cargo ships, outside.
Saw the Terminal Island prison behind you.

And thought, whoa,
this is a challenge . . .
I guess to use the current vernacular—I *leaned* in.
I told you what I could do for you.
And for the next five years, I did.
I ran interference, I organized, I counseled—
I took any job you would give me.
Went anywhere you would send me.

My complaints were when I was excluded from a meeting,
or not given enough work.
That was a long time ago—
but I believe we had a profound effect on each other.

I had to leave my job early,
my health became the problem:
You—the understanding boss.
You were the rock who
was always still there.
But you didn't get to retire.

You received a Presidential Medal of Honor.
You mentored hundreds of people.
But you died, *transitioned to the other side*,
left the planet while still Regional Counsel ICE
(Immigration Criminal Enforcement)

The big C got you even with a fight.
CANCER. This generation's scourge.
I was devastated I could not fly to your funeral.
I was too ill.
I thank my lucky stars I had spoken to you a few weeks before.
I could not believe I was still alive, sick but alive.
Survivors' guilt. Living a half mononucleosis life all these years—
but you were gone.

The few, the strong, the brave, the good, die young.
You hung in till the end.
I will always honor your memory.
I tell countless stories to my daughter, her friends,
about what true integrity looks like.

It's William B. Odencrantz.

© Sharon D. Greenspan, 2014.
William B. Odencrantz passed away in 2009, at the age of 62.

146

SYLVIA'S EULOGY

I have thought over the last few days of all the words for mother:
Mom, mommy, *ema, mater, matajun,*
Sylvia, formerly Sali, Sara *bat* Maita
I know that going forward I will miss calling those words.

In my case, as far as Sylvia is concerned it could be me saying,
"Oh mom, that's so great." "Thanks mom, you're great."
Come on mom, you can make it through another one.
I love you, mom.

I recently realized that her legacy
is that I learned most of those words from *her.*
As my nephew Michael said yesterday,
"Everyone loved her because she made you feel good about yourself."

This past year was extremely difficult,
lots of hospital rooms, procedures, bags, etc.,
but everyone loved Sylvia.
They would walk in her room and say "Sylvia, how are you?"
And she would give them a big wide smile.
Smiles and love are definitely contagious.

She was always up for the next *simcha.*
Made it to all of her grandchildrens' *Bar and Bat Mitzvahs.*
Would have loved to hold on for some weddings,
but that was not to be.
However, when those weddings come,
I am sure she will be there in spirit.

When I was younger, all my friends loved my mom.
Her house was always open for a meal.
She was always there with a kind word.
She'd listen to trials and tribulations
and always have happy, simple words of advice.

Friends who have spoken to me over the past few days,
remembered similar things.
Your mom had such a positive attitude. She was so sweet.

And who could forget those fifty person Seders with the stuffed veal breast?
Her grandchildren loved the matzo ball soup that all *bubbes* are made of.

She was able to take everyone on an adventure, and offend very few.
So I loved my *ema*—I hope I did right by her—
I will miss her—and I hope she is in a happier, peaceful place
with my dad Efraim Fischel and her parents and siblings.

I'm sure there is a Mahjong game, or poker or bingo up there.

Glossary

- **ARBEIT MACHT FREI**. A German phrase meaning 'work makes you free' that was posted at the entrance of concentration camp Auschwitz during the Holocaust, sending the message that it was a labor camp, and not a death camp. (Used in: *Avodah*)
- **avodah**. In Hebrew, this is translated as to stand or to work. (Used in: *Avodah*)
- **bashert**. The Hebrew word referring to something as destiny. This is often used as a term for someone's significant other, implying they are the person they are destined to be with. (Used in: *Ten Aunts and Uncles*)
- **bat**. This is the Hebrew word for daughter, or daughter of. When you refer to a woman or girl's name in Hebrew, you often use their parent's name in the phrase (i.e. Sharon, daughter of Sylvia). (Used in: *Sylvia's Eulogy*)
- **Bat Mitzvah**. A Jewish ceremony for a 12 or 13 year old girl entering adulthood in the Jewish religion. This term is applied to females; the term applied to males is Bar Mitzvah. (Used in: *Those Two Guys, Sylvia's Eulogy, My Post Office*)
- **beh-rim**. 'Let's go' in Farsi, the Persian language. (Used in: *Persian Princess*)
- **Beth Din**. In Hebrew, this refers to the Jewish Court of Law. (Used in: *The Thirteenth Tale*)
- **Bismillah-ir-Rahman-ir-Rahim**. Arabic blessing before eating or undergoing an action, meaning "In the name of G-d, the merciful and compassionate." (Used in: *The World Trade Center: The Tower of Babel*)
- **bubbe, bubbes**. The Yiddish term for grandmother. (Used in: *Sylvia's Eulogy, The Plagues of Pesach*)
- **ema**. The Hebrew word for mother. (Used in: *Sylvia's Eulogy*)
- **Erev Rosh Hashanah**. Hebrew for the eve of the Jewish New Year. (Used in: *The World Trade Center: The Tower of Babel*)
- **ghand**. The term for sugar cube in Farsi or Persian, which is often put between one's teeth. (Used in: *Persian Princess*)
- **haft-seen**. A traditional table setting for Nowruz, the Iranian spring celebration. (Used in: *Persian Princess*)
- **Hashem**. Literally translated as The Name in Hebrew, this is the word often used to refer to G-d, without saying the name in vain. (Used in: *Tante Leah*)
- **hijabs**. Typically worn by Muslim adult females, this is a veil that covers the head and chest. (Used in: *Love in the Time of the Immigration Service*)
- **Hey-lee baad**. 'Very bad' in Farsi, or Persian. (Used in: *Beware of Mentors*)

- **Khoreshts**. A term referring to a Persian stew served at many Persian meals. This can also be spelled Khoresh. (Used in: *Persian Princess*)
- **kippot**. The Hebrew word for yarmulkes, the skullcap worn by Jewish men. (Used in: *Love in the Time of the Immigration Service*)
- **Kristallnacht**. The term for the Night of Broken Glass, a pivotal night during the Holocaust that took place in November of 1938. Jews and their properties were attacked throughout Nazi Germany and Austria, leaving shards of shattered glass throughout the streets. (Used in: *Beware of Mentors*)
- **L'chaim.** Translated from Hebrew as "To Life", this phrase is often used when raising your glass in a toast, or celebrating a happy occasion. (Used in: *My Uncle Jack, The Plagues of Pesach*)
- **L'vorrechecha v'yeeshmarecha, cain yehi ratzon**. A Hebrew blessing meaning 'Bless you and protect you, may it be thy will'. (Used in: *N'shama Chaya for Betty Kogan*)
- **lashon hara**. In Hebrew, this is translated as evil speak, referring to gossip or speaking poorly of another person. (Used in: *N'shama Chaya for Betty Kogan*)
- **machetanim**. The Hebrew term for referring to new family related through marriage. (Used in: *The Plagues of Pesach*)
- **marror.** The Hebrew term for bitter herbs or horseradish, grated on Passover to signify hardship. (Used in: *The Plagues of Pesach*)
- **matajun,** or **matajoon.** Persian word for loving mother or 'Mommy, dear' Adding jun or joon to the end of a name is to add 'dear'. (Used in: *Sylvia's Eulogy*)
- **mater.** German variation for the word 'mother'. See *muter* as well. (Used in: *Sylvia's Eulogy*)
- **meine liebshun**. German for 'my love'. (Used in: *The Name Game*)
- **Merengue**. A Latin or Spanish salsa dance style. (Used in: *By Definition*)
- **muy mala**. 'Very bad' in Spanish. (Used in: *Beware of Mentors*)
- **muter.** German variation for the word 'mother'. See *mater* as well. (Used in: *The Name Game*)
- **N'shama Chaya**. The Hebrew term for a good soul or a woman of valor. (Used in: *N'shama Chaya for Betty Kogan*)
- **Nicht gut.** A German term meaning 'not good' or 'not well'. (Used in: *Beware of Mentors*)
- **Nowruz**. The Iranian or Persian New Year, also marking the first day of Spring. (Used in: *Persian Princess*)
- **Ojibwan.** A member of the Native American tribe Ojibwe. (Used in: *Persian Princess*)
- **Osay Shalom Bim Romav. Who Ya'aseh Shalom Aleinu, V'al Kol Yisrael V'Imru—Amen.** A Hebrew blessing said during the Mourner's Kaddish that

means 'May the one who brings peace in the Heavens bring peace upon us'. (Used in: *Those Two Guys*)

- **Pesach.** The Hebrew term for the Jewish holiday of Passover, also referring to the Paschal lamb sacrifice. (Used in: *The Plagues of Pesach*)
- **Raftam.** Another Persian term for 'Let's go'. (Used in: *Persian Princess*)
- **Sabbath.** The Jewish weekly holiday, observed from Friday sunset to Saturday sunset. (Used in: *Cooked Chickens*)
- **Sabzis.** The Persian term for greens such as fenugreek, wheatgrass or green onions. (Used in: *Persian Princess*)
- **Salaam**. The Persian word for peace. (Used in: *Persian Princess*)
- saris. A garment worn by Indian women that consists of a special fabric draped around the body. (Used in: *Love in the Time of the Immigration Service*)
- **Shalom**. The Hebrew word for peace, also used as 'hello' and 'goodbye'. See Salam above for Persian version of the same word. (Used in: *Persian Princess*)
- **Shalom chaverim**. The Hebrew term for 'Hello, friends' or 'Welcome, friends'. (Used in: *The Plagues of Pesach*)
- **Shema Yisrael Adoshem Echod**. Hebrew phrase meaning "Hear the nation of Israel, one and only G-d," it is part of a prayer said in Jewish daily services. (Used in: *The World Trade Center: The Tower of Babel*)
- **shidduch**. The Hebrew term for the matchmaking set up of two people, or an arranged marriage. (Used in: *Tante Leah*)
- **shiva**. A period of time observed by Jews who have recently endured the loss of a close family member, held at the home of those who have experienced the loss, allowing family and friends to come visit them during their hardship. (Used in: *Cooked Chickens*)
- **shomer Shabbos**. A Hebrew term referring to someone who observes the Sabbath, or the act of observing the Sabbath. (Used in: *N'shama Chaya for Betty Kogan*)
- **simcha; simchas**. The Hebrew word for happy occasions and celebrations, such as weddings, Bar/Bat Mitzvahs, etc. (Used in: *My Uncle Jack, Sylvia's Eulogy*)
- **Tahdigs**. A rice dish served in Persian food that is typically made in a pot from basmati rice and oil, until it becomes crispy. (Used in: *Persian Princess*)
- **Tante**. The Yiddish word referring to Aunt. (Used in: *Ten Aunts and Uncles, Tante Leah*)
- **Timshel**. The Hebrew word for 'Thou Mayest' used in John Steinbeck's book the East of Eden. (Used in: *To John Steinbeck, About Journey of a Novel*)
- **turbans**. A headwrap worn by men from various countries in Asia and the Middle East. (Used in: *Love in the Time of the Immigration Service*)
- **Yahrzeits**. The Jewish observance of the anniversary of a close one's death by lighting a candle to preserve their memory. (Used in: *Those Two Guys*)

- **Yakshemash**. The term for 'How are you?' in Polish. (Used in: *Television is my savior*)
- **Yiddishe mama**. A term used to refer to a Yiddish or Jewish mother. (Used in: *The Name Game, Ten Aunts and Uncles*)
- **Zayde**. The Yiddish word for grandfather. (Used in: *My Uncle Jack, Those Two Guys, The Plagues of Pesach*)

Acknowledgments

No creative work is ever done in a vacuum. This book has been in the process for over thirty years. I acknowledge that I have been afraid to bring it into the light—fear of rejection. Therefore, now that it has been birthed, I would like to acknowledge all those who have supported me along the way.

First, I wish to thank all of the professional caregivers who have helped me to cope with the greatest challenge of my life—chronic fatigue syndrome. They were there when I could not see how to go on. With love and admiration—Dr. Andrea Rentea (and Carla and Nicole), Mei Lu (my acupuncturist), Lois Silverstein MS LCSW, Dr. Michael O'Rourke, Dr. Alexander Prager, the CFIDS Association of America, and my past doctors Jay Goldstein and Jeffrey Galpin. Good deeds are rewarded.

I would like to thank all of my friends and extended family—many of whom don't have a poem about them, but are no less important. Special love and gratitude to Linda S. Fine, Leslie and Michael Salerno, Davya Stewart, Carla White, Renee Bass, Robyn Shutman, Michelle Mazarei, Matajoon Nasrin, Lew Janowsky, the kids Amanda, Paul, Tim, Bijan and Piaj. Then my card girls: Mag, Jan, and Mick. My Latinas, Martha, Blanca, Griselda and Ione. At my deepest, darkest hours you have all been there for me.

Thank you to all of my Shir Hadash family—for standing by me—especially Rabbi Eitan, Melanie, Susan, Bonny, Lynne, and Diane.

Thank you to my family, even though at times you don't know what to do—both of my brothers, Jay and Jeff and sisters-in-law B.J. and Eleanor. To my nieces and nephews: Eva and Michael (and spouses Zach and Brooke), Jered, Jason, Rachel, Sophie, Ben and Dan, I love you all. Shoshana, the door to my heart is always open to you.
Thank you to all of the authors at all of the book signings over the years who have encouraged me to—just do it!

But thank you the most to my lovely cousin-niece, Hillary Marshak Preston, for seizing the opportunity and making this book a reality. Working with such a wonderful, living human being has been a present.

Lastly—my Samantha—the world lights up when you enter a room. God blessed me when he gave me you as my daughter. Love to my parents, and the rest of my family on the other side.

All my love,
Sharon D. Greenspan

153